IN

THE

WAITING

Spice Lyfe

Preface

Since I was a young girl, I've had a story to tell. Writing; [whether on paper or in my head] has always been my great escape. Words have power and my desire is that the power of the words I write bring hope and manifest new beginnings for every reader. Every encounter in my life, whether good or bad, has inspired me in some way to be a greater version of me.

I pray that this book and those to come, inspire each reader the same way, which leads me to acknowledge a few of the inspirers of my journey thus far.

Dedication

Saije Mckynzie is not only the greatest human inspiration in my life, she is also my greatest reason to consistently seek and walk in my purpose. She is my biggest cheerleader and my most prodigious accomplishment. I simply marvel at every conversation. Every moment spent. And every effort [successful or otherwise] she brings. I adore you daughter and I appreciate you Loving me through my challenges as your mother. You are my reason 365 days a year. This book particularly allows me to write to you all the things that I had to learn the hard way about being single in hopes that you will not have to endure the same.

God gave me you to push me to my greater

me. I love you.

My siblings and all of your offspring and

significant others. Jimmy [Dawn and kids].

Angelia [kids and grandkids]. Rodney.

Wakeef [kids]. Santana [kids]. Reginald [Step,

kids, and grandkids]. Regina [B, kids, and

grandkids]. Rique [Nicholle, kids, and

grandkids]. Tammy [child]. You guys are my

everything. I am everything that I am

because of the push of encouraging words

and abundant love you guys give. I truly

thank you. Gordon's, Johnson's, Mitchell's,

William's, and Jackson's forever. Good days

and bad days are still the best days when we are all together. I love you guys. I thank the amazing people that God put in myself and Saije's life for divine purpose. My blood parents didn't tarry long on Earth yet God saw fit to bless us with so many more; offering the purest love a girl could ask for. The Ballard's [Tyson and Tayden]. The Rumble's [Jackie and Roddy]. The Howard's. The Pruitt's. Mother Janet [Will]. Also, to Latoya [kids], Jerneisha [my lil sis], Rock [Tamiko], and Kay [RdBlcc]. All of you guys became god-parents, grandparents, aunts and uncles and cousins to my daughter and I *and we are both eternally grateful. Love you guys.*

All of the relationships [on every level] I have ever had; each inspired every word in this book. Thank you all for helping me rewrite the narrative of a wayward [deviating from what is desired, expected, and required] thinking! I love and tremendously appreciate every experience...farewell.

And finally, to the three most important people when it comes to this book coming to life... The woman that said on 3/18/22, "...What are you doing in the waiting...uuummm...that's a book." Pastor Sheree' Evans of the Faith Room/ The Lady's

Room. The person that requested to stay

anonymous and blessed me with the funds

to publish this book [I Love you so; family

over everything]. You two have no idea the

impact you made on my life in these two

moments. My ex-husband; my friend Justin

Woodard for your contribution to publishing.

When I mentioned to someone that you had

offered the blessing their response was,

"Hahaha...he paying to make sure you don't

say anything bad about him..." Of course, I

defended your honor and told them how

awesome you are and that I didn't have a

bad thing to say about you either way.

Thank you Mr. Woodard! Tears well up even

now as I think on you three. May God give you all back 800-fold the blessings you have been to me.

The real push behind writing this book was the pain endured by yet another failed relationship that forced me to see ME. In the midst of finishing up this book for publishing this man that I thought was my end game passed away. We spent the first quarter of 2022 together and life was perfect. He was my perfect. We parted ways on a positive note to better ourselves and one day live our happily ever after whether together or with someone else; we just both understood that we both had some things we needed to work on before sharing our lives with another

human being. He set the standard for a good

man. He defied the odds of a black man. He

was my friend and I will Love him forever.

This one is for you Corrie Antwon High

"MyHigh".

Smitty P aka CD4E Loves you and will

forever keep our amazing memories alive.

Without further ado; I now give birth to "In

The Waiting" through birthing pains and with

the purest Love...Thank you!

Table of contents:

The Waiting

The Divorce:

*****Selah: Pause for refelction*****

The Waiting

The waiting can be likened to many areas of life. In this book, the waiting is referenced as the time taken as a single individual to prepare the mind, body, and spirit to become in union with a spouse.

Now, if you're anything like me; At an early age, you did everything you were big and bad enough to do, including premarital sex. So, honey, when you learn what the word says and now you have to abstain...wwwooohhh chile that "wait" hits different! I mean, truth be told, we were getting it in around my way in middle school, *so imagine not learning truth until a decade later. Better yet, imagine not submitting to that truth until not one, not two, but three decades later! Guilty!*

*But hey, my faith tells me in **Romans 8:1** There is therefore now no condemnation to them, which are in Christ Jesus, who walk not after the flesh, but after the Spirit. So, imagine after all the failed relationships, broken hearts, playing the fool, trying to figure out what's wrong with you or the way you love...only to now come into submission and not be able to love or be loved for a season of waiting?*

Well, shugg let me tell you, and bear with me

as I try my hardest not to cuss while

expressing the growing pains of the waiting

season.

You see, God showed me a long time ago the

calling He had for my life. Talk about the

prodigal son. Honey this daughter ran from

God to the world and back again, so much it

was bananas.   That internal fight with your

love for God and your lust for the world is

heavy. And if you're honest with yourself, the

world wins some days. Now imagine the

wait where the worldly lusts have no place.

It is like a forced fast from all things that

keep you from walking in your Godly

purpose, including your relationship as a

husband or wife.

The Bible doesn't spend much time telling us

about Adam waiting, but I imagine it was so

bad that God himself looked down and said

let me give this dude some body. However,

let us not forget when Jacob had to wait for

Rachel only to be lied to and have to wait a

total of 14 years. In those times life was

different and multiple wives was a heavy

thing so some wouldn't consider Jacob really

in the waiting but imagine sleeping with a

woman that you had absolutely no attraction

to for 14 years because you were forced to

marry the oldest sister first. Jacob did what

was required for his first true Love until the wait was over. So, men; fathers in this day and age are not requiring of you to marry the oldest sister first but God is requiring that you have some boxes checked to be in His will as a husband.

Ladies, ladies, ladies...How many women of God are in this here Bible that were in waiting? Sarah waited 90 years for a baby. Ruth waited with her mother-in-law, laying at smelly feet. But honey, most of us are like that other daughter-in-law of Naomi's named Orpa. We throw up the deuces saying,

"Alright then, I'ma head out. Wait on who to do what for who? Nah!"

*That wait is a beast ready to devour your flesh and spit out a new you. The You God intended for you to be. Who is that? Glad you asked. Men, according to the **Book of Titus**, around about Chapter 2 God intended for you to be level headed, worthy of respect, sensible and sound in faith, love and endurance, and consistently making yourself an example of good works with integrity and dignity in your teachings. Who are you teaching? Your brothers, sons, grandsons, nephews, cousins, neighbors, strangers, and coworkers by being the example of men of* valor when it comes to defeating the enemy through your lifestyle and character. So, in summary, men of God here are some scriptures for you to meditate on in the waiting. **Deuteronomy 8:3** Nourish yourself with the word. **Ecclesiastes 12:13** Reverence God. And keep his commandments. **1 Corinthians 11:3** Know your position. **Ephesians 5:25** Know how to love a wife before you take a wife. **1 John 2:9-11** Remove the darkness of hate and malice.

OK, ladies, now let's get in formation. Who and what does Daddy G tell us to be as women of God? So, round about **Titus 2** as well; it states that we should be reverent in behavior not slanderers (cackling hens) Not addicted to much wine...help me, Lord. Teach what is good. Teach who...glad you asked. Our sisters, daughters, granddaughters, nieces, cousins, neighbors, strangers, and coworkers. Love your husband, love your children, be self-controlled, pure (never too late to reset...as long as sink water can be purified then so can you no matter your past!). Homemaker does not mean you can't work. Be submissive to a husband who first submits to God. So now that we know what a man and woman of God are to be, let's dive into how to get there...back there for some of *us. Hello, somebody! And stay there for all of*

us. Selah and turn the page.

The Divorce

What is divorce? Well, in the marital rim, divorce is the legal dissolution of a marriage by a court or other competent body. However, in the waiting, we are going to look at divorce in the aspect of a verb which states to separate or dissociate something from something else. According to some studies, there are five different stages to divorce.

*1. **Denial.** Funny thing is, most of us look at denial as a refusal to accept the thing. Yet this particular study I read describes denial as being incapable of processing what's happening. So, shock if you will. Sometimes we are even in shock at assessing situations* and seeing what we have allowed. The initial once over you do of your life for whatever period you choose to assess without the blinders of your past, lust, love, and fears can leave you speechless at what you have allowed for so long. From self and others, and let's be clear... others include parents, children, friends, siblings, employees, spouses, etc. The list truly goes on. Shake the shock and start the process

2. **Anger**. That feeling that makes you say to self...IKYL. Just mad at everything. Who or whatever that thing that your spirit is immensely trying to free you from makes you angry about everything, even when it is not

coming from a bad place. Everything. This is

who and or what angers you, whether

positive or negative. Truth be told, the

positive angers you more because the

positive goes against the battle to divorce the

who or what? Here is the nugget. We must

remember with anger, **Ephesians 4:26** *tells*

us to be angry, but sin not. Well with anger,

being a passion, which is defined as a strong

and barely controllable emotion; then how on

earth can I be angry and sin not?

Self-discipline. Don't lose a blessing from the

burdens of your anger. Selah and keep

reading.

3. **Bargaining.** *Bargaining according to this study, is known as the "What if" stage. Bargaining makes us say things to ourselves like, "It's my mom. She knows what's best." "My dad will always show me what's right." "My kids come first." "But we've been friends since the sandbox." "Blood is thicker than water." "I need this job." Or how about that horrible one we have all heard our whole lives... "Having a piece of man is better than having no man at all." Bargaining is a heavy one to grasp, so allow me to provide scripture for clarity of each example and to give mental armor to the battle that is consistently in our minds. So, let's get into it. What does the*

word say about my relationship with my parents? Now don't misunderstand me; as a matter of fact, as the old saying goes, read 10 up and 10 down from the scriptures I share throughout this book and get your own knowledge and understanding. I'm just planting the seed. Now let's be clear, many scriptures point to honoring thy mother and father etc. but are we clear that honor doesn't mean adhering to their ways if they don't align with God's word? **Ezekiel 20:18** states not to follow the statutes of your father's, defile yourselves with their idols, or keep their ordinances. So, you see those traditions and/or choices because "I had no other *choice; this is all I know" goes out the door.*

*Then there is **Matthew 10:34-39** where*

Daddy G tells us that he did not come to

bring peace on earth, but a sword to turn

man against his father, daughter against her

mother, daughter-in- law against her

mother-in-law, and a man's enemies will be

members of his household. The person who

loves his father or mother more than me is

not worthy of me. The person who loves his

son or daughter more than me is not worthy

of me.

So, you see, sis, your kids don't come first.

Well...we still in the waiting, so that chain of

command is for another season and a

different book. But understand the headship

of God, man, wife, and child.

And let's keep growing.

Being loyal to family members that treat you

like Joseph? According to **Proverbs 27:10** *it*

is better a neighbor nearby than a brother far

away. I mean; let us not forget that Cain

killed Abel. Blood is thicker than water, but

has nothing to do with you staying loyal to a

family that would sell you to the highest

bidder or slaughter you as soon as jealousy

and strife enters into their hearts. How about

staying on a job that is not conducive to your

purpose nor spirit, but you're chasing a

dollar. A man or woman not in the right

position, even on a job, is out of alignment in their whole life. Let's be clear, money is good and needed yet the Bible has been so misquoted with people stating that money is the root of all evil. Money is necessary, however, according to **1 Timothy 6:10**, which states for the LOVE of money, is a root of all evil and by chasing it, some have wandered away from the faith and pierced themselves with many pains. So, you see that job you holding onto, or better yet, that bag you're chasing in any capacity...chase God like that and trust that **Matthew 6:33** which tells us to seek yea first the Kingdom of God and his righteousness, and all these *things shall be added unto you, Selah. And*

keep reading.

I'd rather have a piece of man than no man

at all. HoneyBaby Betty Wright messed up a

whole generation or two with this one. If I

had to put Scripture with it, it would have to

*be **2 Timothy 2:22** which states flee from*

youthful passions and pursue righteousness,

faith, love, and peace along with those who

call on the Lord from a pure heart. You see

the youthful passions that we pursue after

had us accepting anything from the person

that had our soul at that time. A little time, a

few gifts, a few meals, and plenty of sex

would have us accepting a piece of time in

someone's life; knowing the time we didn't have was shared with someone else.

On the other hand, a person pursuing righteousness, faith, love and peace and they call on the Lord from a pure heart...now that is the person that will give to you their whole life. That is the person that would do anything to be your everything. So let us not settle for a piece of man or woman my sisters and brothers, but let us; in the waiting become the good thing that he finds and the righteous husband that she honors.

Even without Scripture, we can make sense of why a piece of man or woman does not make sense. Check it. Piece is defined as a portion of an object or of material produced by cutting, tearing or breaking a whole. Pieces are meant to be shared; in example piece of cake, piece of pie, piece of pizza, piece of candy, etc. The only sharing we should be doing with our spouses is sharing them with God and our children (whether made together or brought together in union with a blended family). Everything and everyone else have no place unless it is ministry or business and even then, the headship still remains in order. Divorce bargaining. Now Selah and keep reading.

4. **Depression.** I think we miss being able to identify depression when we've invited it in

*for a sit down in our minds because we
assume depression only looks a certain way.
Well let's explore the idea that depression
can take on many forms in our lives; I mean
how many stories have we all heard of the
person that committed suicide seeming to be
overly happy and unbothered? And while we
can all agree that "normal" looks different for
some more than others the reality is there is
a foundation of "normal" that we should be
cautious of when unseen. For example, I saw
on a board at a restaurant and I quote,
"Outwardly I'm nonchalant, but inside I'm
chalant af." Wow, right? Can you relate? Or
do you know someone that can? So, let's take*

that for example...sometimes people are

constantly repeating things; not as an

affirmation of encouragement, but as a

repeated way to try and convince the internal

battle to cease in their mind. It is their way of

yelling "STOP" without looking schizophrenic

outwardly. The need to insistently tell the

world something that internally you are still

trying to convince yourself of is a big red flag

to start paying attention to your mental

health without shame. We must be cautious

of the fine line between insistently and

incessantly; because once you cross over you

could possibly be stepping into your first

stages of depression. Be vulnerable enough

to let down all guards and do the work to help improve your mental health and or go get help to improve your mental health. Your state of mind is vital to being your best you and dealing with all things "Life" especially in the waiting.

5. **Acceptance.** AAhhhhh the arrival to the freedom from internal turmoil! The stage we all desire to be after pain. Remember not to beat yourself up if some around you gets there sooner than you. Always keep in mind that your time in the waiting is about YOU and no one else. Your healing, your learning, your growing; so be sure to take YOUR time in getting to this stage but don't tarry long. In

the words of my cousin-sister-girlfriend

Cathy Wilkins, "Stay encouraged; keep

pushing and when you get to life's peak you

hang on to your blessings. New beginnings

are always knocking. Love CatMae"

So, once you know you have fully arrived at

the level of acceptance by journeying through

these 5 stages you can begin to self-check

when conflict arises. You see; how you

handle conflict is a direct reflection of your

mind-set and discipline level. At this point

you get to look in the mirror and say, "Have I

really forgiven? Am I really over this pain?

Am I really ready to give Love a try again?

Am I..." and fill in the blanks of self-check

that you know needs to be answered in that

mirror. Selah and turn the page.

Part one:

Childhood

The reality that this chapter forces us to face isn't pretty, but not only is it ugly; It is reminiscently painful of all the things from childhood that helped form who we are today. However, now is the time; in the waiting to face it all and divorce the things from our childhood that for years has kept us in deep covenants with the demons assigned to keep us bound from our purposes, fulfillment, and destiny.

The pains of neglect, abuse, molestation, rape, incest and premature exposure, to name a few are the very enemies that have us mentally, spiritually and intentionally imprisoned.

So, let's get into it and rewrite the narrative of what was put in place by principalities to stop our purpose.

Besides all of the ugly things that happened to us in our youth, the one that holds the most power is the "sweep it under the rug" secrecy that continues to allow history to repeat itself. History in syllables is broken down to his-story. In order for his story [the molester, abuser, etc.] not to become the next generations curse, we must acknowledge the

demonic thoughts and actions that plague us,

our parents, our uncles, cousins, aunts, and

friends; we must be the ending and the new

beginning. Re-writers of the narratives that

yoke us out of our assignments.

After reading this chapter; my prayer is that

you take a moment [and let that moment be

as long as it needs to be] and remember all

the things that you can from your childhood.

Make a list of the pros and cons. Then study

the list of cons and find the lessons learned

from each experience. The lessons are the

catapults to the next level of you! Learn from

them, grow from them, and stop being a child

posing as an adult because you can't let go of what happened. But instead; become a better you by using what happened and rewriting the narrative of the rest of your life and the generations after you. We all know that we cannot change what happened but do we all also know that we can't dictate the justice given [or not given]? Do we truly understand that those battles are not ours? Do we truly know how to cast our burdens upon the Lord? If we are being honest with self; then not always. However, the following are some scriptures to help when we do not have the courage and fight to help ourselves. **Psalms 34:18** tells us the Lord is close to the brokenhearted. **Psalms 147:3** tells us that

He binds up wounds. **2 Corinthians 1:3-8**

tells us that He comforts us. **1 Peter 4:12-19**

tells us to rejoice in the suffering because we

are inflicted in His name and therefore

blessed with the resting of His Spirit upon us.

This is just a few of the many scriptures that

will help through overcoming the trials of our

past traumas. Take some time and read

them and find more to meditate on daily and

or as often as needed to help.

Now Selah and turn the page.

These people. These people that did what they do and produced you. These people that are supposed to love and protect you. These people that are supposed to direct and guide you, nurture and define you; these people. Two humans that possibly did their best by you or their worse; because it was done to them. Fellas; the lady that you first loved. Ladies, the man that first loved you or was supposed to. **Proverbs 1:8-9** tells us to hear our father's instructions and to forsake not our mother's teaching, for they are the *graceful garland for your head and pendants*

for your neck.

I know some of you guys have to be thinking God was tripping when he inspired Solomon to write this proverb with the parents God gave you. But let's be clear, if we are going to believe God makes no mistakes, then we have to believe there is purpose even in those parents that were or are not so parenty. I can only speak for myself when I say some of my greatest lessons come from the not-so-great circumstances. Hints my push to write this book in 3 months' time.

So, let's go. Let's run down some of the lifestyles, traditions, circumstances and thought processes embedded in us from

these people we call Mom and Dad.

As a matter of fact, let's go back to one I

already touched on.

Was it not our parents that taught us that

blood was thicker than water? It got so

embedded in our beliefs that the very blood

they taught us to respect and be loyal to are

the very ones that hurt us...FAMILY. Then we

do things like sweep truths under the rug by

the direction of the parents. They want us to

cover up horrible truths from our blood that

have the power to mentally, physically, and

spiritually cripple us for a lifetime and

generation after generation.

But how many of you know that our parents were crippled as well? So, after you find it in your hearts to forgive them; be sure to forgive yourself for all the years of disrespect you showed or the alt you held in your heart for blaming them for something that they did not realize was not normal. Divorce their ways that have enabled so many for so long...Selah and turn the page.

Peer can be misleading as assuming it only refers to those being equal in age. When in fact; peer is defined as not only equal in age but equal in skill or other categories. So, the first thing this tells me is to choose my peer group wisely. But how many of us haven't always? DIVORCE! Leave those peers behind that whether intentionally or unintentionally mean your purpose no good! Peer pressure is a real thing so your peer group is very important. The type and force of pressure that they apply is equally important to your purpose. "Yes Friends" aren't always the best friends and "No friends" aren't always the haters. Beware and don't let your "Yes Friends" yes you straight out of your purpose on a slow fall to hell shouting YESSSSS!

If the old saying holds true; that you are the average of your 5 closest friends, then this means 2 peers follow you, 2 peers lead you, and 1 is wishy washy. This does not mean the 2 that follow cannot teach nor does it mean the 2 that lead cannot learn. It does however mean that if either side is not enhancing your purpose, then they are enabling your purpose and must be DIVORCED.

Proverbs 27:6 *tells us that wounds from our FRIENDS are faithful yet kisses from our ENEMIES are deceitful. So, keep a watchful eye on those that say yes to everything, every idea, every outfit, every relationship, etc. Do not let the truth that a real friend tells you trigger your insecurities into you thinking they are hating. The real haters are those that see you on a slow fall to hell and yes you into jumping on into the lake of fire.* *Proverbs 27:17* *tells us that iron sharpens iron, so a friend sharpens a friend. Selah and turn the page.*

Part 4:

Sex Partners/Exes

*Baby, let me tell you, when I first got blessed with the VHS tape, No More Sheets by Juanita Bynum! Man listen; changed my life for a quick season [before my first encounter with backsliding]. Shoot; I wasn't brought up in church, but once I started going and seeing how church folks was living, I thought how I was living was normal in the sight of God. Until he put Oris Pruitt in my path. That man of God is **2 Timothy 3:16-17** in the flesh. Just rebuking, correcting and training and I thank God daily for his assignment over my* life (along with the many others that keep me aligned even when I don't want to be). Love and appreciate you all!

Anyhow, honey when Juanita came on stage with them sheets wrapped around her and taught us to divorce all the people we had slept with, I felt that thing. You hear me? I felt it long enough to abstain for a season, but not stay there. However, the seed was planted and has continued to grow even when my butt just kept marrying more sheets. Sheesh. You'd think that all the heartache would stop me from trying; but the hope for a genuine love kept me looking the wrong way for a spouse. Yeah, I do my little *detox from people and sex hiatus but just as soon as an old dream selling guy came along, I'm right back boo'd up and praying that this time is the right time. The desire from youth that planted lust all up in my spirit just kept winning sheet after sheet.*

Relationships within themselves are hard to navigate so imagine putting all of our worldly lusts, worldly expectations, and unequally yoked choices in the mix.

*I went through my "hippie" stage of life where loving (whether physically intimate or not) whoever was the freedom in being a free spirit. However, **Galatians 5:13** tells us that we have been called to live in freedom but* not to use this freedom to satisfy our sinful nature but instead to serve in love. Boy did I have that scripture all wrong out here living like a butterfly. I laugh now as I thank God I made it through without a life sentence but oh the pain that comes with giving yourself to the wrong people. So, imagine the divorce to break those soul ties...NOT EASY because do not mistake it...them soul ties come with lots of sinful fun! But the path of destruction never ends good if we do not divorce those that are not meant to be yoked to our purpose.

The following nugget is the best thing I have ever done for myself and I make sure to do it *after every "divorce" DETOX! Even if you fall short again...DETOX!*

I acknowledge that every reader of this book may or may not be actively participating in fornication, so I will intensely encourage for all sides. So, you are either saving yourself for your mate, resetting to save yourself for your mate, or just not active [until you are again]. Either way, take the necessary time to detox from the previous situation. In that time focus on you! Pause from sex and defeat the urge to indulge. The pause is not a promise of the provision of your happily ever after. However, in your pause season also known as the waiting; give all that you have into being your greatest version of you. Then,

when God manifests the provision of Love

you are fully capable of being a good

steward that behaves with high morals,

accountability, and all the things needed to

be the man or woman God calls you to be as

a spouse. Brad L. Austin said it best,

"Analyze life to understand how to do things

better and more proficient for your next

relationship." Purge in the waiting all of the

ole' faithful's and prepare yourself for your

destined one.

Selah and turn the page.

Part 5:

Me, Myself, and I (All Of Em')

Genesis 1:26-27 tells us that God said we were made in His image...male and female He created us. So, what does that say to you personally? For me it says that if we were created in His imagine then our lifestyle should reflect Him. Honey believe me....my nose turned up too! No, not at God but at the struggle of trying! On the one hand you have the PK's (Preacher Kids) and RK's (Regular Kids...my own Ebonics) that were brought up in church and taught by the word. Some stay the course and some go astray. The ones that go astray get a taste of sin and honeybaby...

Then on the other hand you have the RK's

that only attended church once a year on

Easter, only when they visited with family

and friends that attended church, or were

never even introduced to God, Jesus, and the

Holy Spirit until young adulthood...ME and

many like me; where sin was the everyday

norm. It's crazy how each side is fighting to

get to the other side. The saints love to sin

and the sinners just want a better life; and

no matter what side you are on; ain't none of

it looking like God and His image.

Well life is gone keep on lifing no matter what

choices we make or the choices that were

made for us and so here we are...Me, Myself, and I. You, Yourself, and You. The product of all you have ever known. The evidence that life happens around your way. The result of every choice you have ever made. What do you think of you? Do you like you? Love you? Accept you? Every detail? Let me be the first to tell you that if you have made it to the mindset that all of your answers are YES then you have stopped growing and we should be forever growing until our last breath. You have stopped living and life will devour you whether soon or later. The mirror is nonexistent and you can't see the mess of you to clean it up; to divorce it and marry the

next level of you.

The daily thought process should always have the goal in mind to be a better version of you today than you were yesterday and hope to make it to the greater version of your tomorrow. No matter if you are a spouse, a parent, or caretaker; you will always first be an individual person that must not depend on others to approve you, make you happy, dictate your life, etc. Latoya Odom said it best, "...When you depend on people to build you up, they'll have the same power to break you down. You don't need their validation to know your worth."

Do you know your worth? Did you know that just like the value of anything else; the value of you can depreciate? So, you must do the work to keep your worth in the running's. What does doing the work look like? Glad you asked.

*Let's start with the past. LEARN FROM IT AND LEAVE THE PAST BEHIND YOU. Past hurts, past mistakes, past people. Nothing in life has happened to you; perhaps it has happened for you. DIVORCE the past! The Word tells us in **Isaiah 43:18-19** to remember not the former things, to not consider them at all, and to behold for the new thing!*

***Matters of the heart**...HEAL! Easier said than done; I know. Yet without healing you are just an open wound walking around bleeding your painful blood on the world especially innocent kids that aren't born with unforgiveness but taught unforgiveness through your pain. Innocent kids that don't know promiscuity but are taught it through your actions while you are looking for love in all the wrong sheets. Innocent kids that are taught to fight, shoot, and kill their own people because of your own insecurities and desires to be accepted and respected at all cost. Deciding to go through the healing process can be scary; however often times* *the very thing that you fear doing is that very*

thing that will set you free when you do it.

*HEAL and stop bleeding. Repeat **Psalm***

***51:10** daily...hourly if you have to as a*

friendly reminder to Daddy G to create in you

a clean heart and renew in you a right spirit.

***Matters of your health**...RESET! Let me*

take a moment and say I had to laugh with

God when He nudged my spirit with this

piece because I have been able to diligently

do the work in all areas that I write about

except this...this struggle is harder than

falling into fornication for me and if you know

me honeybaby that can be a struggle but I'm

yet holding on! Pray for me; hear? Anyhow,

what God showed me is that in writing this book I am vulnerably allowing all of my readers to hold me accountable and now I must go harder staying the course! So, thanks Daddy G for that pressure...as I do a childish eyeroll!

In health, the first thing we must understand is that every diet does not do the same to every body. And let's be clear; the definition of diet is the food and drink that you regularly consume; not something you do just to lose weight. So, what is your diet? Is it working for your health? Is it nourishing every essence of your being? Is your gut healthy? Do you experience inflammation?

After you take a moment and answer these questions about yourself; take the next moment and ask yourself...say, "Self, do we need to divorce our diet?" For me the answer was YES! When I tell you my gut is jacked up from gas I mean that thing. My momma; God rest her sweet soul used to say, "Girl you ain't gone ever get no man with all that gas in yo tail!" Now if you knew my momma you know she used a different word at the end but I told you all to bear with me and my cussing spirit. Now you know where I got it from.

Shout out to my oldest, sweet sister Angelia that did the work to improve her health and *like an awesome big sister would do, she shares with me all the things I need to know to be my healthiest version of me...and honeybaby I tried it all. Consistency is my enemy but I'm taking back dominion over my health and I suggest you all join me! And here is what the Word says we can eat: In **Genesis 1:29** He gave us every herb bearing seed and every fruit of the trees. Then in **Genesis 9:3-6** He gave us every moving thing that lives as meat. Later in **Leviticus** and **Deuteronomy** He tells us what is clean and unclean. Finally in **Mark 7:18-22** Jesus declared all food clean stating that we are defiled by what is in our hearts and not our* stomachs because it can be dispelled. So back to my original statement...Every diet does not work the same for every body. Find which works for your body. Say your Grace. Eat. Workout. Repeat. Selah and keep reading!

Matters of the Mind...Now how many of you can relate; whether for self or someone you know about being mentally trapped in a house with unlocked doors and open windows? Joyce Meyer tried to set us free with her book Battlefields of the Mind but here we are still in the same repetitive battles. An internal turmoil that cannot be described and can hardly be defeated.

What are your internal battles? Have you jotted them down? Do you acknowledge them at all? Have you allowed those mental battles to become a normal and make a home in your mind? Well good brother and my darling sister; how long will you tarry looking out of the open windows and not walk out of the unlocked doors?

Life is waiting for you to make a move. People are waiting for you to get in position. Your purposed self is waiting for you to align with your purpose and a significant piece of that puzzle is your mate.

***Becoming ONE**...Now **Proverbs 18:22** tells us that he who finds a wife finds a good* thing. Then **Ephesians 5:25-29** tells husbands to love their wives as Christ loved the church. So, ladies we must ask ourselves, "Am I a good thing?" Fellas, you must ask yourselves, "Am I ready to give myself up for a wife?"

The answer starts with, "Have I done the work on myself..." because honeybaby; being a spouse is way deeper than knowing how to cook, clean, pay bills, and as my momma would say it, "screw!" There is a mental shift from single to union that must happen before we say "I do."

It's not about buying your own house, buying your own ring, or being able to do for yourself *in any capacity. It is; although you can do it for yourself; are you now able to be in a union and make sound, respectful, and responsible choices as One? Are you able to be lead and still be a learning leader? Are you able to be lead while still learning? Are you ready for the blended family you signed up for? Are you capable of forgiving? Are you ready?*

As I close out, I would like to leave a few scriptures to really meditate in preparation to being in a union. As we do the self-work, here are two phenomenal nuggets for keepsakes: my Bible study group leader gave this one...changed the way we see P.Y.T.

forever! Bind this nugget to your daily thoughts and do it as often as you breathe. In the words of Minister Melinda Douglas, "Create the space to hear from God and discern his voice...P.Y.T. Prayer, Yield, and Time. Pray often. Yield to His voice. Spend time in His Word."

I don't know about you but I'm absolutely exhausted with choosing the wrong mate and being chosen by the wrong mate. I need to "PYT" before I even go on a date now! If it isn't for me, I DO NOT WANT IT!

This last one is a quote by author Erin Van Vuren that is **HEAVY**! *Bind this to every essence of your being and remember every* *time someone even looks in your direction...unless God says yield...* **"I will not be another flower, picked for my beauty and left to die.**

I will be wild, difficult to find, and impossible to forget."

Selah

A few scriptures needed to understand being One:

Ephesians 5:33

Proverbs 3:3-4

Romans 12:10

1 Peter 3:7

Matthew 19:4-6

1 Peter 4:8

Ephesians 4:2-3, 32

Hebrew 10: 24-25

Ecclesiastes 4: 9-12

Understand Love by **1 Corinthians 13: 4-5.**

Understand submission by **Ephesians 5:21.**

Read the whole book of **Song of Solomon**

before you make Love ever again!

Selah and thanks so much for reading!

~Spice~

Epilogue

This book was written in a place of chosen solitude to 'do the work.'

"The Wait is Over" will be written in a place of union when God allows me to become One with who He has especially for me. Stay tuned.

And always remember, no one can truly Love who you are when they only get to see who you present yourself to be.

Many blessings and appreciation to you all!

By the way, this blessed gem is not the only good thing birthed in Raleigh, NC...If you ever come through be sure to book with William's Way Airbnb (my dope middle sister Regina and her hubby Big B got you), shop with Crimey Dealers (the homies Clock and Kutta gone have whatever you need), book with Eccentric 360 Vibez for the photobooth, cop you some of that good ole sea moss from my sistergirlfriend Machon Banks, get the dopest fade from the homie Tony at Billionaires Barbershop, and so much more in this little city we call Raleigh-Wood.

Blessings and Peace

All scripture references taken from different versions of the Holy Bible, KJV, NIV, and Apologetics.

King James Bible. (2008). Oxford University Press. (Original work published 1769)

The Holy Bible: New International Version. The Gideons International in the British Isles, 2012.

Apologetics Study Bible for Students. Holman Bible Pub, 2014.